The ANCIENT GREEKS

THE ANCIENT GREEKS

VIRGINIA SCHOMP

Marshall Cavendish
Benchmark
New York

~ *For Paul Tesnakis* ~

The author would like to thank John Paulas of the University of Chicago
for his valuable comments and careful reading of the manuscript.

Benchmark Books Marshall Cavendish 99 White Plains Road Tarrytown, New York 10591-9001
www.marshallcavendish.com Text copyright © 2008 by Marshall Cavendish Corporation All rights reserved.
No part of this book may be reproduced or utilized in any form or by any means electronic or mechanical,
including photocopying, recording, or by any information storage and retrieval system, without permission
from the copyright holders. All Internet sites were available and accurate when this book was sent to press.

LIBRARY OF CONGRESS CATALOGING-IN-PUBLICATION DATA Schomp, Virginia. The ancient Greeks / Virginia Schomp.
p. cm. — (Myths of the world) Summary: "A retelling of several key ancient Greek myths, with background
information describing the history, geography, belief systems, and customs of the ancient Greeks"—Provided
by publisher. Includes bibliographical references and index. ISBN-13: 978-0-7614-2547-2 1. Mythology,
Greek—Juvenile literature. 2. Greece—History—To 146 BC—Juvenile literature. I. Title. II. Series.
BL783.S39 2007   398.20938—dc22   2006028375

EDITOR: Joyce Stanton   ART DIRECTOR: Anahid Hamparian
PUBLISHER: Michelle Bisson   SERIES DESIGNER: Michael Nelson

PHOTO RESEARCH : Rose Corbett Gordon

Images provided by Rose Corbett Gordon, Art Editor, Mystic CT, from the following sources:
Cover: Cameraphoto/Art Resource, NY Back cover: Vanni Archive/Corbis Pages 1, 41, 88: Art Resource,
NY; pages 2-3, 24, 73, 83, 85: Scala/Art Resource, NY; pages 6, 8, 21, 36, 43, 50, 65: Erich Lessing/Art
Resource, NY; page 7: David Lees/Corbis; pages 10-11: Stapleton Collection/Corbis; page 12: British
Museum/HIP/Art Resource, NY; page 15: Vanni/Art Resource, NY; page 17: Mary Evans Picture
Library/Minos Collection/The Image Works; page 18: Krause, Johansen/Archivo Iconografico, SA/Corbis;
page 19: Bildarchiv Preussischer Kulturbesitz/Art Resource, NY; pages 26 (top), 38, 40: Réunion des
Musées Nationaux/Art Resource, NY; pages 26 (bottom), 27, 72: AAAC/Topham/The Image Works; pages
28-29: The Philadelphia Museum of Art/Art Resource, NY; pages 30, 32, 37, 42: Bridgeman Art Library;
page 34: Fine Art Photographic Library/Corbis; page 35: Archivo Iconografico, SA/Corbis; page 44:
Trustees of the Royal Watercolour Society, London, UK/Bridgeman Art Library; pages 46, 48: The British
Museum/HIP/The Image Works; page 51: Bibliotheque des Arts Decoratifs/Bridgeman Art Library; pages
53, 66: The De Morgan Centre, London/Bridgeman Art Library; page 55: Leeds Museums and Galleries
(City Art Gallery) UK/Bridgeman Art Library; pages 56, 59: Louvre, Paris, France/Bridgeman Art Library;
page 58: Heritage-Images/The Image Works; page 60: Christie's Images/Corbis; page 62: Mary Evans
Picture Library/The Image Works; pages 64, 90: Tate Gallery, London/Art Resource, NY; pages 68, 70, 76,
79: Mimmo Jodice/Corbis; pages 74, 90: The State Russian Museum/Corbis; pages 78, 89: Gianni Dagli
Orti/Corbis; pages 81, 89: The Art Archive/Corbis; page 82: Araldo de Luca/Corbis; page 84: National
Gallery Collection, By kind permission of the Trustees of the National Gallery, London/Corbis

Printed in Malaysia
135642

Front cover: Ariadne, Aphrodite, and Dionysus, in a 16th-century painting by Tintoretto
Half-title page: 1st-century BCE bronze figure of Eros
Title page: Detail from *The Fall of Icarus* by Italian artist Carlo Saraceni (about 1579–1620)
Back cover: Poseidon, Apollo, and Artemis, sculpted on a wall of the Parthenon, a famous temple
    of the goddess Athena built in the 5th century BCE.

CONTENTS

THE MAGIC *of* MYTHS

EVERY ANCIENT CULTURE HAD ITS MYTHS. These timeless tales of gods and heroes give us a window into the beliefs, values, and practices of people who lived long ago. They can make us think about the BIG QUESTIONS that have confronted humankind down through the ages: questions about human nature, the meaning of life, and what happens after death. On top of all that, myths are simply great stories that are lots of fun to read.

What makes a story a myth? Unlike a narrative written by a particular author, a myth is a traditional story that has been handed down from generation to generation, first orally and later in written form. Nearly all myths tell the deeds of gods, goddesses, and other divine beings. These age-old tales were once widely accepted as true and sacred. Their primary purpose was to explain the mysteries of life and the origins of a society's customs, institutions, and religious rituals.

It is sometimes hard to tell the difference between a myth and a heroic legend. Both myths and legends are traditional stories that may include extraordinary elements such as gods, spirits, magic, and monsters. Both may be partly based on real events in the distant past. However, the main characters in legends are usually mortals rather than divine beings. Another key difference is that legends are basically exciting action stories, while myths almost always express deeper meanings or truths.

Mythology (the whole collection of myths belonging to a society) played an important role in ancient cultures. In very early times, people created myths to explain the awe-inspiring, uncontrollable forces of nature, such as thunder, lightning, darkness, drought, and death. Even after science began to develop more rational explanations for these mysteries, myths continued to provide comforting answers to the many questions that could never be fully resolved. People of nearly all cultures have asked the same basic questions about the

Four of the mighty gods and goddesses of ancient Greece. *From left to right*: Poseidon, Athena, Apollo, and Artemis.

Opposite: A fashionable Greek woman of the 5th century BCE

The one-eyed Cyclops played an important role in ancient Greek stories about the origins of the gods.

world around them. That is why myths from different times and places can be surprisingly similar. For example, the peoples of nearly every ancient culture told stories about the creation of the world, the origins of gods and humans, the cycles of nature, and the afterlife.

Mythology also served ancient cultures as instruction, inspiration, and entertainment. Traditional tales offered a way for the people of a society to express their fundamental beliefs and values and pass them down to future generations. The tales helped preserve memories of a civilization's past glories and held up examples of ideal human qualities and conduct. Finally, these imaginative stories provided enjoyment to countless listeners and readers in ancient times, just as they do today.

The MYTHS OF THE WORLD series explores the mythology of some of history's greatest civilizations. Each book opens with a brief look at the culture that created the myths, including its geographical setting, political history, government, society, and religious beliefs. Next comes the fun part: the stories themselves. We based our retellings of the myths on a variety of traditional sources. The new versions are fun and easy to read. At the same time, we have strived to remain true to the spirit of the ancient tales, preserving their magic, their mystery, and the special ways of speech and avenues of thought that made each culture unique.

As you read the myths, you will come across sidebars (text boxes) highlighting topics related to each story's characters or themes. The sidebars in *The Ancient Greeks* include excerpts from a variety of ancient sources, including poems, histories, a hymn, and a dialogue (a work written in the form of a conversation). The sources for the excerpts are noted at the back of the book. There's lots of other information at the back as well, including a glossary of difficult terms, a biographical dictionary of Greek writers, suggestions for further reading, and more. Finally, the stories are illustrated with both ancient and modern paintings, sculptures, and other works of art inspired by mythology. These images can help us better understand the spirit of the myths and the way a society's traditional tales have influenced other cultures through the ages.

Now it is time to begin our adventures in ancient Greece. We hope that you will enjoy this journey to a land where wondrous gods rule from the mountaintops and superhuman heroes perform daring deeds. Most of all, we hope that the sampling of stories and art in this book will inspire you to further explorations of the magical world of mythology.

ΗΦΑΙΣΙΟΣ   ΔΙΟΝ

ΞΟΣ   ΚΩΜΩΙΔΙΑ   ΜΑΡΣΥΑ

Part 1

MEET *the* GREEKS

The GREEK LANDSCAPE

THE ANCIENT GREEKS LIVED IN SOUTHEASTERN EUROPE, around the Aegean Sea. Their homeland included what is today the country of Greece, which is located on the Balkan Peninsula and many nearby islands. The Greeks also established settlements across a broad area that extended north and east to the Black Sea and Asia Minor (present-day Turkey), west to parts of Italy and Sicily, and south to the African coast.

The landscape of mainland Greece is rugged and mountainous. Only about a quarter of the rocky countryside is suitable for farming. Because of the shortage of natural resources, the people of this region have always depended heavily on the sea. Since ancient times the Greeks have fished in the coastal waters and sailed the seas to trade with settlements on close-lying islands and distant shores.

The natural environment helped shape the stories told by the people of ancient Greece. Many of the Greek myths were set against a

Opposite: Ancient ruins on the coast of Athens, Greece, overlook the Aegean Sea.

Previous *page:* Dionysus, god of wine, with his followers in a sacred procession

THE GREEK WORLD AROUND 500 BCE

ITALY

CUMAE

SICILY

THE BALKAN PENINSULA

BLACK SEA

MACEDONIA

MT. OLYMPUS

GREECE

MT. PELION

MT. PARNASSUS

AEGEAN SEA

ELEUSIS

ATHENS

OLYMPIA

MYCENAE

SPARTA

DELOS

PAROS

ICARIAN SEA

SAMOS

ICARIA

TROY

ASIA MINOR

KNOSSOS

MT. IDA

CRETE

MEDITERRANEAN SEA

AFRICA

EGYPT

AREAS OF GREEK INFLUENCE

N

MILES

0   100

KILOMETERS

0   100

Poseidon, god of the sea, drives a chariot drawn by marvelous part-horse, part-fish beasts known as hippocampi.

background of mountains, caves, and seas. The mountains of mythology were wild, mysterious places where divine beings roamed. Most sacred of all was Mount Olympus, Greece's highest peak, whose snow-capped crown held the palaces of the great Olympian gods. Mountain caves might be the birthplace of a god or the lair of a savage beast. The myth "In the Beginning" on page 31 describes the birth of Zeus, king of the Olympians, in a cave on the island of Crete.

According to Greek mythology, the seas were home to a number of different deities, all ruled by the mighty Olympian god Poseidon. The waters were calm when this unpredictable god was happy, but his anger could bring crashing waves and deadly peril for sailors. To learn how Poseidon's temper gave the world a terrible, flesh-eating monster, see "The Birth of the Minotaur" on page 64.

$\mathcal{A}$ GLORIOUS HISTORY

POLITICAL HISTORY ALSO PLAYED A ROLE IN THE development of the Greek myths. The first great civilization of ancient Greece emerged around 3000 BCE, on the island of Crete. This ancient culture is known as Minoan, after its mythical founder, King Minos. According to one traditional tale, Minos was a son of the god Zeus. The king's magnificent palace in the city of Knossos on Crete was the setting for several myths, including "Theseus and the Minotaur," retold on page 57, and "Daedalus and Icarus," page 69.

While the Minoans flourished on Crete, another civilization was developing on the Greek mainland, centered in the ancient city of Mycenae. The warlike people of the Mycenaean civilization lived in huge fortress-cities ruled by powerful kings. Around 1400 BCE the Minoan civilization declined, and the Mycenaeans became the dominant power on Crete. As the cultures of these two great civi-

The figure in this painted wall sculpture from the palace of Knossos on Crete may be Minos, the mythical king who gave the Minoan civilization its name.

lizations mingled, the Minoans' ancient stories of gods and other supernatural beings found new life in Mycenaean tales.

In time the Mycenaean civilization also faded. Some historians think that the decline was caused by foreign invasions, while others believe that Mycenaean society was torn apart by conflicts among its warrior kings. Whatever the cause, Greece entered a long period of upheaval known as the Dark Age. Throughout these troubled times, the ancient Minoan-Mycenaean tales were preserved through the poetry and songs of wandering minstrels.

Around 800 BCE a new Greece emerged, made up of many small mainland and island communities. The people of these scattered settlements developed an alphabet and began to write down their ancient tales in imaginative histories called epic poems. The first of the Greek epics were the *Iliad* and the *Odyssey* by Homer. These famous poems describe events surrounding the Trojan War, a great conflict between the Mycenaean Greeks and the ancient city of Troy. Parts of the long tale of the Trojan War are retold on page 77.

In the fifth century BCE, Greece entered an era of wealth, power, and accomplishment often called the Golden Age. Hundreds of Greek city-states, or poleis, had been established across the Mediterranean world. Each polis had its own independent government and traditions. While the people of the Greek city-states were politically divided, they all shared the same basic language, along with many of the same religious beliefs and myths.

Philip II, king of Macedonia, conquered Greece in the 4th century BCE.

The Golden Age came to an end in 338 BCE, when the Greek city-states were conquered by Philip II, king of Macedonia. Under Philip's leadership the independent poleis joined together in a united federation. Philip's son, Alexander the Great, led that federation in a ten-year military campaign, building the largest empire the world had ever known. Wherever his armies claimed victory, from Egypt to India to Afghanistan, Alexander founded cities modeled on the Greek city-states.

After Alexander's death in 323 BCE, the power of Greece slowly faded. In its place rose the mighty Roman Empire. The Romans admired and imitated Greek culture. By spreading the traditions, beliefs, art, and mythology of ancient Greece throughout their vast empire, they preserved its heritage for future generations.

Alexander the Great spread the culture of ancient Greece across a vast empire.

A variety of systems of dating have been used by different cultures throughout history. Many historians now prefer to use BCE (Before Common Era) and CE (Common Era) instead of BC (Before Christ) and AD (Anno Domini), out of respect for the diversity of the world's peoples.

GOVERNMENT *and* SOCIETY

OVER THE COURSE OF THEIR LONG HISTORY, THROUGHOUT all their city-states, the ancient Greeks had many forms of government. At different times and places, the Greek people were ruled by chiefs, tyrants, groups of nobles, and kings. In the years leading up to the Golden Age, the world's first democracies took root in Greece. The strongest and most important democratic government was founded in the city-state of Athens. Other Greek city-states also set up democracies, many copying the Athenian model.

The people of a democratic city-state were not all considered equal. Strict rules determined which members of society were entitled to the rights of citizens. In Athens, for example, only free men over the age of twenty who had been born to Athenian parents could vote in the Assembly, the governing body that decided on public policies. At age thirty, Athenian citizens gained the right to serve as jurors and help make laws.

Beneath the privileged upper class in Greek society was a large group of foreign residents known as *metics*. Members of the *metic* class often worked as merchants, craftsmen, manufacturers, doctors, teachers, or in other skilled trades. While *metics* might earn great riches, they were usually forbidden to own land, and they had no political power.

The third and lowest class was made up of slaves. Even the poorest citizen or *metic* owned at least one slave, while rich households might own as many as fifty. Slaves had no political rights. Some masters allowed their slaves to live and work on their own, in return for a share of their wages. Slaves who earned enough money were sometimes able to purchase their freedom.

Greek wives and mothers were honored in their homes, and they played an active role in some religious celebrations. However, women of all classes were largely excluded from the public life of the city-

A young Greek woman at home, holding a mirror in one hand and turning to face the viewer. Behind her an open door gives us a glimpse of her bed. From a 5th-century BCE vase painting.

The Olympians battle giants and goatlike satyrs on the ceiling of a 16th-century palace in Mantua, Italy.

was Zeus, ruler of the sky and earth. Zeus shared his power with his brother Poseidon, lord of the sea. He had three sisters: Hera, who was also his wife and queen of the immortals; Hestia, goddess of the hearth; and Demeter, goddess of agriculture. Also seated on the thrones of Olympus were seven of Zeus's children: Athena, Aphrodite, Apollo, Artemis, Ares, Hephaestus, and Hermes. Some sources include Hades, ruler of the underworld, in the list of Olympian gods. The Family Tree on page 27 shows the connections among the Olympians and their special areas of power and responsibility.

DAILY DEVOTION

WORSHIP WAS AN IMPORTANT PART OF DAILY LIFE IN ancient Greece, both for individuals and for the entire community. The Greeks offered regular prayers at altars in their homes. They also worshipped at shrines, sanctuaries, and temples scattered across the countryside, from caves to crossroads to mountaintops.

At special times throughout the year, all the people of a city-state joined together to celebrate religious festivals. These elaborate ceremonies often began with a grand procession to the temple of the god or goddess who had been adopted as the patron deity, or special protector, of the polis. At the temple worshippers honored the deity with prayers, music, dancing, and gifts of food, wine, and sacrificial animals.

A few festivals united all Greeks in worship. The highlight of these Panhellenic (Greek-wide) festivals were the athletic competitions.

Above: Animals were sacrificed at ancient Greek festivals honoring the gods.

Below: Boxers compete on a 4th-century BCE vase.

Thousands of people gathered to watch as athletes from every polis strived to honor and impress the gods with their skills in running, wrestling, discus throwing, chariot racing, and other sports. The most famous Panhellenic festival was held every four years at Olympia, a center for the worship of Zeus. This glorious celebration was the inspiration for our modern Olympic Games.

Wherever and whenever the Greeks gathered, their age-old myths were there. At home parents instructed and entertained their children with the traditional tales of gods and heroes. Men relaxing in the marketplace or the Assembly traded songs and stories based on mythological themes. At religious festivals and other public gatherings, myths were recited as poetry or acted out as plays. To the ancient Greeks these time-honored tales were more than good stories. They were a living, ever-present part of life.

FAMILY TREE *of the* OLYMPIANS

The most important Greek deities were the twelve gods and goddesses known as the Olympians. Some sources include Hades in this list, even though his home was the underworld rather than Mount Olympus. Later lists sometimes add Dionysus, the popular Greek god of wine and merriment.

POSEIDON
God of the sea

HESTIA
Goddess of
the hearth

DEMETER
Goddess of
agriculture
and fertility

ZEUS
King of the
Olympians;
god of the sky
and earth

HERA
Wife of Zeus;
goddess of
marriage

APOLLO
Son of Zeus and Leto,
a Titan; god of light,
poetry, music,
and science

ARTEMIS
Daughter of Zeus
and Leto; goddess
of the hunt

ATHENA
Daughter of Zeus
and Metis,
a Titan; goddess of
war, wisdom, and
the arts

HEPHAESTUS
Son of Zeus and
Hera; god of fire
and artisans

APHRODITE
Daughter of Zeus
and the goddess
Dione, *or born from*
the flesh of Cronus;
goddess of love
and beauty

HERMES
Son of Zeus and Maia,
a Titan; messenger
of the gods

ARES
Son of Zeus
and Hera;
god of war

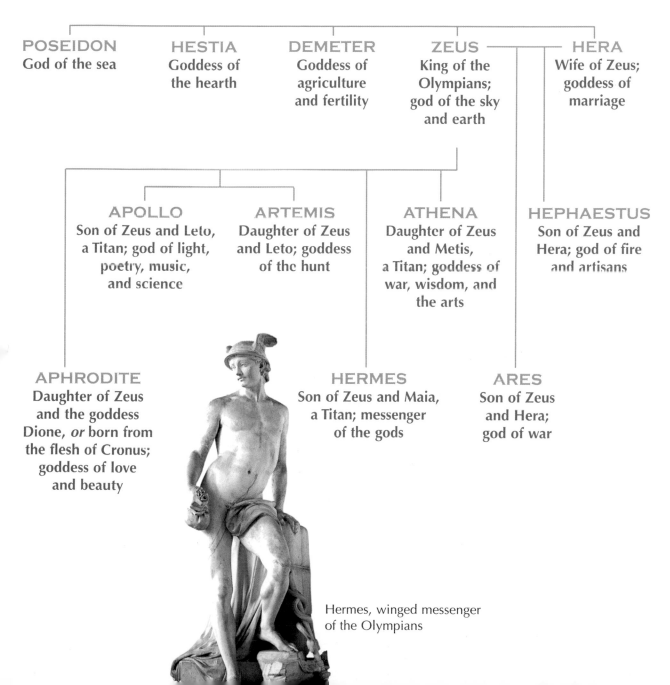

Hermes, winged messenger
of the Olympians

Part 2

TIMELESS TALES of ANCIENT GREECE

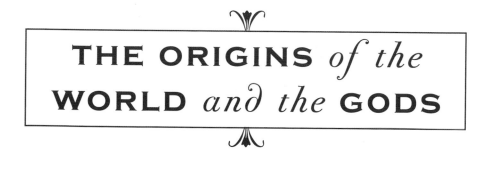

THE ORIGINS *of the* WORLD *and the* GODS

In the Beginning

LIKE ALL ANCIENT PEOPLES, THE GREEKS TOLD MANY stories about beginnings. Some Greek myths explained the origins of particular cities, social groups, and customs. Some dealt with the beginnings of humanity. Still others reached all the way back to the creation of the world and the birth of the gods.

Because myths were passed down orally, growing and changing with each retelling, there are often many different versions of the same story. This version of the Greek creation myth comes mainly from a long poem called *Theogony* ("Genealogy of the Gods"), written by the poet Hesiod around the eighth century BCE. Hesiod based his poem on a variety of traditional stories. He organized and connected these age-old tales to come up with a grand narrative that traced the development of the world all the way from an empty void to an orderly society controlled by the gods. *Theogony* described the struggle among three generations of gods and the triumph of the Olympians. It was one of the most popular and influential literary works of the Golden Age, inspiring countless poets, playwrights, historians, and philosophers.

Opposite:
The Cyclopes were fearsome one-eyed giants who crafted lightning and the thunderbolt.

Previous page:
Listeners pay rapt attention to one of Homer's tales in this scene painted by 19th-century artist Lawrence Alma-Tadema.

CAST *of* CHARACTERS

Mother Earth First goddess of the earth; also known as
Gaea (JEE-uh)

Eros One of the creative powers of the universe

Father Sky Ruler of the first generation of gods; also known
as Uranus

Cyclopes (SIE-klah-peez) One-eyed giants

Hundred-Handers Monsters with fifty heads and one hundred arms

Titans Twelve immortal children of Earth and Sky

Cronus (KROW-nus) Ruler of the second generation of gods

Rhea (REE-uh) Wife of Cronus

Zeus (zoos) Ruler of the third generation of gods

I N THE BEGINNING there was nothing but a vast shapeless Void.
Out of the Void emerged Mother Earth, along with Eros, the creative force that moves gods and men to desire. When Earth felt the
touch of Eros, she grew lonely. So all by herself she produced a husband, who was named Father Sky.

Sky was a perfect fit for Earth, covering her on all sides with his
great starry blanket. Out of their union came many remarkable chil-

dren. There were three Cyclopes, gigantic creatures with a single eye in the middle of their foreheads. There were three Hundred-Handers, horrid monsters with fifty heads and a hundred arms sprouting from their shoulders. But the boldest of all were the twelve immortal giants called Titans.

Mother Earth loved all her children, no matter how big and ugly. But Father Sky looked upon his monstrous offspring with fear and horror. He bound the Cyclopes in chains and cast them down into Tartarus, the deepest part of the underworld. He sent the monstrous Hundred-Handers to the same gloomy region. For the bold Titans, he dreamed up an even crueler fate. As each of these immortal children was born, Sky stuffed it back inside Earth, where it twisted and turned, tormenting its mother.

At last Earth could take no more of Sky's heartless behavior. She begged her children to help her take revenge on her husband. At the thought of confronting their mighty father, all the children were seized with a paralyzing fear—all, that is, but the youngest Titan, Cronus.

Mother Earth was delighted with her son's brave spirit. She made a long, jagged sickle and gave it to Cronus. She hid him in a dark corner of her bedchamber. Soon Sky came once again to cover Earth with his starry blanket. This time Cronus was ready. With a slash of the saw-toothed blade, the young Titan sliced off his father's private parts and tossed them into the sea, stripping the god of his limitless power.

After Cronus conquered Sky, he sent the wounded god into exile. Then he took his father's place as ruler of the world. Cronus freed his fellow Titans from bondage and married his fair-haired sister Rhea. In time Rhea bore six splendid children: Hestia, Demeter, Hera, Hades, Poseidon, and Zeus. But, like his father before him, Cronus loathed his children. Through a dreadful prophecy, he had learned that he was

The BIRTH *of* APHRODITE

In Hesiod's version of the Greek creation story, the wounding of Father Sky leads to the birth of Aphrodite, goddess of love and beauty. Here the poet describes what happened after Cronus threw Sky's private parts into the sea.

White foam issued from the divine flesh, and in the foam a girl began to grow. . . . She stepped out, a goddess, tender and beautiful, and round her slender feet the green grass shot up. She is called Aphrodite ["foam-born"] by gods and men, because she grew in the froth. . . . Eros [Desire] and beautiful Passion were her attendants both at her birth and at her first going to join the family of the gods. The rights and privileges assigned to her from the beginning and recognized by men and gods are these: to preside over the whispers and smiles and tricks which girls employ, and the sweet delight and tenderness of love.

Above: Aphrodite rises from the sea, in a 19th-century French painting.

destined to lose his throne to his son, just as he himself had overthrown Father Sky. So the king of the gods kept a sharp watch, and as each one of his immortal children was born, he swallowed it whole.

Rhea grieved long and hard for her lost children. Finally, as the birth of her sixth child drew near, she begged her parents for help. Mother Earth and Father Sky were moved by their daughter's sad story. Together they contrived a scheme to conceal their grandchild's birth. Under the cover of darkness, they sent Rhea to the island of Crete. There Zeus was born in a deep, dark mountain cave. Leaving the infant in the care of the mountain nymphs, Rhea rushed home to her husband. She wrapped a huge stone in baby clothes and gave it to Cronus. The poor fool believed that the bundle was his newborn son. Grabbing the stone, he quickly gulped it down into his belly.

This gruesome image of Cronus devouring one of his children was created by the celebrated Flemish painter Peter Paul Rubens.

The seasons passed, and young Zeus grew in size, strength, and wisdom. It wasn't long before he was ready to face his cruel father. Once again Mother Earth came to her grandson's aid. Using honeyed words, the cunning goddess persuaded Cronus to retain the handsome youth from Crete as his personal servant. She helped Zeus prepare a mixture of salt and mustard. The young god stirred the potion into a cup of sweet nectar and gave it to his father. Cronus drained the cup in a single gulp. His belly began to roll and rumble. Suddenly the great god

Rhea presents Cronus with a wrapped stone instead of baby Zeus.

vomited up the stone he had swallowed years before. Then, one by one, Cronus threw up his children.

Rejoicing in their freedom, the immortal children of Cronus went to live on towering Mount Olympus. Soon a terrible war raged in the heavens. On one side were the gods of Olympus, with Zeus as their leader. On the other side were Cronus and the Titans, who swore that they would never yield power to the young rivals. For ten long years the enemies fought without ceasing. Finally, Zeus traveled down to Tartarus, the dark underworld where Father Sky had imprisoned the Cyclopes and the Hundred-Handers. He freed the monsters from their gloomy dungeons, earning their undying loyalty. The grateful Cyclopes forged thunder and the lightning bolt and gave these to Zeus to make him master of gods and men. The Hundred-Handers, dreadful and strong, pledged to join the Olympians in their fierce struggle with the Titans.

That very day a grim battle began, involving all the gods and monsters. The earth quaked and the mountains trembled as the two sides collided. Loud battle cries rose to the heavens, and the sound of pounding feet sank all the way to Tartarus. At the very front of the battle lines, the Hundred-Handers hurled huge boulders, which rained down on the Titans in a deadly shower. Then Zeus revealed his full power. Charging through the skies, the great god cast lightning and thunder, blinding his enemies and enclosing them in a whirlwind of fire.

MOUNT OLYMPUS TREMBLED FROM BASE
TO SUMMIT AS THE IMMORTAL
BEINGS CLASHED.

~HESIOD, 8TH CENTURY BCE

At that, the battle turned and the mighty Titans were overpowered. Binding their fallen enemies in chains, the Hundred-Handers carried them far below the ground to Tartarus. There the Titans dwell to this day, in a region so dark and dismal that even the gods grow pale when they hear its name mentioned.

With their rivals safely imprisoned, the sons of Cronus drew lots to divide up the rule of the world. Poseidon won dominion over the sea. Hades drew the vast underworld as his kingdom. To Zeus went the rule of the heavens and the broad surface of the earth. And, in recognition of his superior power and wisdom, Zeus was also appointed lord of all the immortals.

The ORIGINS of HUMANITY and MISFORTUNE

Prometheus the Fire Giver

AND

Pandora's Box

THE GREEKS TOLD SEVERAL DIFFERENT STORIES ABOUT the origins of humanity. In some early tales, the first men simply sprang up out of the ground. According to other accounts, the gods made men from divine materials or from dirt. But the most popular myth gave the credit for creating mankind to Prometheus.

Prometheus, whose name means "forethought," was a Titan. In the great battle of the gods, he foresaw the fall of the Titans and decided to fight on the side of the Olympians instead. As a reward Zeus spared Prometheus and his brother Epimetheus, or "afterthought," when the defeated Titans were imprisoned in the underworld. The brothers were even entrusted with an important task, the creation of all mortal creatures, including man.

Opposite: An ancient Roman sculpture portrays Prometheus as a master craftsman turning out pint-sized men.

Prometheus was not only the creator of mankind but also its greatest champion. In his best-known myth, the Titan defied Zeus to bring men the gift of fire, one of the essentials of civilization. This act of rebellion against authority made Prometheus a favorite subject for artists, philosophers, poets, and playwrights. One of the most famous retellings of his story was the play *Prometheus Bound,* traditionally said to have been written by the Greek playwright Aeschylus sometime in the fifth century BCE. This dramatic masterpiece showed the noble Titan bravely enduring a horrible punishment for putting the good of mortal men above the will of the gods.

Closely connected with the Prometheus story was the myth of Pandora's box. According to this ancient tale, the first woman was created by the gods to punish man for accepting the gift of fire. Before Pandora's creation, the world was a paradise. With her arrival on earth came all the evils that have plagued humankind ever since. The story of Pandora not only explained the troubles of the world but also justified the dominance of men over women in ancient Greece.

CAST *of* CHARACTERS

Zeus (zoos) King of the Olympians
Prometheus (pro-MEE-thee-us) Titan who was the champion of mankind
Epimetheus (ep-ih-MEE-thee-us) Foolish brother of Prometheus
Hephaestus (hih-FESS-tus) God of fire and artisans
Pandora First woman

Prometheus the Fire Giver

THERE WAS ONCE A TIME when there were no mortal creatures, only gods. From his golden throne on Mount Olympus, Zeus commanded Prometheus and his brother Epimetheus to fill up the vast empty world. Together the two Titans created a host of creatures to populate the land, sea, and air. Then Prometheus took clay, kneaded it with water, and made man. This last creation was also his finest, because it was formed in the image of the gods. Unlike all the other creatures, man walked upright, gazing not down at the earth but up to the starry heavens.

Prometheus flees Mount Olympus with the precious gift of fire.

After the task of creation was completed, Epimetheus persuaded Prometheus to let him deal out all the gifts mortal creatures would need to survive. To some animals he gave sharp claws and teeth. To others went fur for warmth or a thick hide for armor. The busy Titan gave out size, strength, speed, and all the other faculties for preservation. But Epimetheus, who was not so wise as he might be, forgot to leave something for man.

When Prometheus came to examine the distribution, he was sorely troubled. How could he protect his favorite creation? Only one gift remained, one surpassing all the others. This was the gift of fire. But Zeus had decreed that men should never have fire, because that would make them too much like the gods. For an instant Prometheus hesitated. Then, moved by his great love for mankind, the Titan chose to defy the almighty god.

THE ORIGIN
of the SEASONS

Demeter and Persephone

ONE OF THE MOST HONORED GREEK DEITIES WAS Demeter, goddess of agriculture. In mythology Demeter wandered the earth searching for her daughter, Persephone, after the girl was kidnapped by Hades, god of the underworld. During her wanderings, crops withered and died. When the girl was restored to her mother, the earth blossomed again. To the people of ancient Greece, this tale of death and rebirth explained the cycle of the seasons.

The Greeks honored Demeter and Persephone with a festival known as the Greater Eleusinian Mysteries, held each fall in the city of Eleusis, west of Athens. People came from all over the Greek world to join in this important celebration. Because the participants were required to take a vow of secrecy, we have only a general idea of what happened during the Mysteries. We know that the festival began with

Opposite: Persephone and her mother, Demeter, share a fond conversation. This is an unusual ancient Greek statue, because some of the original colors can still be seen.

they completed the temple, the goddess sat down inside it. And there she stayed, still yearning for her lost daughter.

Now came a cruel year for humankind. Demeter would not make the seeds sprout in the ground, and the green earth turned brown and barren. Zeus looked down from Mount Olympus and saw that the entire race of humans was threatened with starvation. He sent a messenger to Demeter, asking her to restore the earth's fruitfulness, but the angry goddess refused him. After that, all the gods and goddesses came, one by one, begging Demeter to return to Olympus. Still she refused, declaring that the world would never know another harvest until her eyes once again beheld her daughter. Finally, Zeus relented. Sending Hermes as his messenger to the dark underworld, he ordered Hades to release Persephone.

The king of the dead smiled grimly when he heard his brother's command. Without a word he harnessed the horses to his golden chariot and handed the reins to Hermes. Then Hades called for Persephone. All this time the shy young bride had sat without eating or sleeping, pining for her mother. Now she sprang up rejoicing. As she mounted the chariot, Hades asked her to think kindly of the husband who so dearly loved her. With a gentle sigh and a sly glance over his shoulder, he gave Persephone a juicy red pomegranate for her journey. For the cunning god knew that those who taste the food of the dead can never return to the land of the living.

The black steeds charged from the palace of Hades. Swiftly the chariot flew through the air to Demeter's temple in Eleusis. When the goddess saw her dear child, she rushed forth and embraced her. But as she held Persephone in her arms, her heart was seized with a sudden misgiving. Fearfully Demeter asked her daughter if she had tasted any food in Hades' dark kingdom. And the girl, in her innocence, assured her mother that she had eaten only one seed of a pomegranate.

Demeter's heart sank. Then, in his wisdom, Zeus issued a new command that would satisfy both mother and husband. Persephone would spend one-third of each year in the kingdom of the dead with Hades and the other two-thirds in the world of light with her mother.

Consoled by this ruling, Demeter flew over the barren earth, causing the flowers to bloom and the fields to swell with grain. Next she went to Celeus, king of Eleusis, and taught him

her sacred rites. Then the goddess returned to Mount Olympus, where she and Persephone rejoiced in the company of the immortals.

And so it is that Demeter brings us the seasons. For when Persephone dwells in the house of Hades, Demeter puts on her dark cloak and the earth is plunged into winter. But when Persephone returns to her mother, Demeter's joy brings the springtime, and the wide world awakens with fruits and flowers.

Persephone returns to earth. The young goddess's reunion with her mother will bring spring to the wintry world.

HEROES and MONSTERS

Theseus and the Minotaur

MANY OF THE MOST POPULAR AND ENDURING GREEK myths concerned the adventures of heroes. Mythological heroes were extraordinary mortals who used their fantastic strengths and talents to perform amazing tasks. Along with their superhuman abilities, they often had very human faults. In their triumphs and tragedies, they experienced many of the same emotions, conflicts, and challenges as ordinary people, only on a much grander scale.

The heroes of Greek mythology usually had at least one immortal parent. The gods played an active role in their lives, either aiding or opposing their quests. While there were a few Greek heroines, most heroic mortals were men. However, women often inspired a hero's adventures or helped him perform his great deeds.

The hero Theseus was sometimes said to have two fathers: Poseidon, god of the sea, and Aegeus, a mortal king. Theseus's most

Opposite: Theseus slays the bloodthirsty Minotaur.

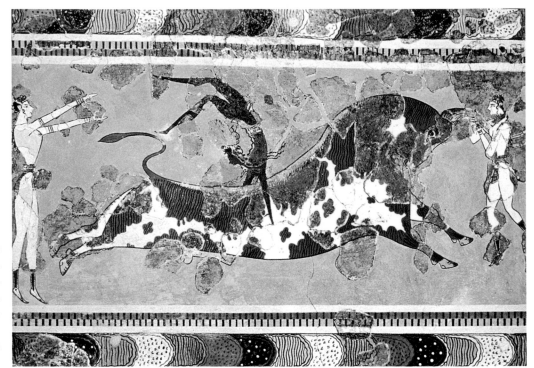

A painting in the palace at Knossos on Crete shows the Minoans taking part in an ancient ritual known as bull leaping.

famous adventure took place on the island of Crete, in the days of Minos, the mythical founder of the Minoan civilization. Minos was a powerful king with a nasty problem. His wife had given birth to a hideous man-eating monster known as the Minotaur. The king confined the Minotaur in the Labyrinth, a vast maze beneath his palace. Every nine years he forced the people of Athens to send a tribute of young men and women to feed to the beast. Theseus ended the tribute and proved his heroic strength and courage by killing the Minotaur.

The story of Theseus's triumph over Minos offered a mythological explanation for the fall of the Minoans and the rise of the civilizations of mainland Greece. To the people of ancient Athens, the myth also explained the founding of their city-state and its democratic form of government. Our version of this popular tale comes largely from a collection of biographies known as *Plutarch's Lives,* composed by the Greek writer and moralist Plutarch around 75 CE.

CAST *of* CHARACTERS

Aegeus (EE-jee-us) King of Athens; mortal father of Theseus

Pittheus (PIT-thoos) Grandfather of Theseus

Aethra (EE-thruh) Mother of Theseus

Theseus (THEE-see-us) Athenian hero

Poseidon (puh-SIE-dun) God of the sea; immortal father of Theseus

Medea (muh-DEE-uh) Sorceress and wife of Aegeus

Minos (MIE-nus) King of Crete

Aphrodite (af-ruh-DIE-tee) Goddess of love and beauty

Ariadne (ar-ee-ADD-nee) Daughter of King Minos

Daedalus (DED-uh-lus) Master craftsman and inventor

Dionysus (die-uh-NIE-sus) God of wine

KING AEGEUS OF ATHENS was weighed down with troubles. He had been married twice, but he still had no son to inherit his throne. So Aegeus went to visit his wise friend Pittheus, the governor of a southern city. And Pittheus gave the king his only daughter, fair Aethra, to love.

When the time came for Aegeus to return to Athens, he led Aethra to a huge boulder. The king placed his sword and sandals in a hollow beneath the rock. Then he gave Aethra a command. If she gave birth to a son who grew up worthy and strong, she must bring him to this spot. If the boy could lift the boulder and retrieve the hidden tokens, she should send him to Athens. All this must be done in great secrecy. For Aegeus had many enemies who would gladly murder the king's heir to secure the throne for themselves.

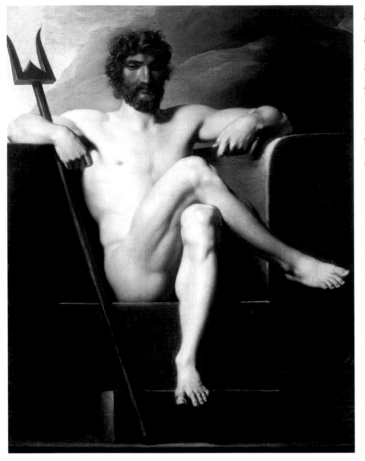

Poseidon, lord of the sea, may have loved fair Aethra. In this 18th-century painting, the god holds his three-pronged spear, or trident, which he used to stir up storms and earthquakes.

In the course of time, Aethra had a son and named him Theseus. Remembering Aegeus's warning, she concealed the boy's identity by claiming that his father was Poseidon, god of the sea. To this day there are some who say that her story was true. Some even say that Aethra was loved by both Aegeus and Poseidon, so that Theseus had two fathers, one mortal and one divine. Whatever his true parentage, the boy grew up strong and bold. When he reached manhood, his mother took him to the boulder. Theseus lifted the heavy rock with ease and found the hidden sword and sandals. Then Aethra revealed the strange story of his birth and told her son to take the tokens to Athens.

There were two routes to Athens: the easy journey by sea and the more dangerous passage along roads infested with robbers and murderers. Theseus's mother and grandfather begged him to take the safer path, but the young man longed to prove his strength and courage

The GLORY *of* HERCULES

For the heroes of Greek mythology, the most important goal in life was glory. Nearly every action taken by a heroic mortal was inspired by the desire to earn glory through brave and noble deeds. Plutarch tells us that Theseus took the hazardous route to Athens out of admiration for Heracles, the most glorious of all Greek heroes. In his story Plutarch refers to Heracles by his Roman name, Hercules.

[Theseus], it seems, had long since been secretly fired by the glory of Hercules, held him in the highest estimation, and was never more satisfied than in listening to any that gave an account of him. . . . In the night his dreams were all of that hero's actions and in the day a continual emulation [jealous ambition] stirred him up to perform the like. Besides, they were related, being born of cousins. . . . He thought it therefore a dishonorable thing, and not to be endured, that Hercules should go out everywhere, and purge both land and sea from wicked men, and he himself should fly from the like adventures that actually came in his way; . . . not showing . . . the greatness of his birth by noble and worthy actions. . . .

With this mind and these thoughts, he set forward with a decision to do injury to nobody, but to repel and revenge himself on all those that should offer any.

The BIRTH *of the* MINOTAUR

Archaeologists investigating the ruins of the ancient palace at Knossos on Crete have found many images of the bull, a sacred animal to the people of the Minoan civilization. It is possible that Minoan priests wore bull-head masks during religious rituals, a practice that may have inspired the tale of the Minotaur. Mythology offered a more fantastic explanation for the monster, as described in this passage by the first-century BCE Greek historian Diodorus Siculus.

> It had been the custom of Minos annually to dedicate to Poseidon the fairest bull born in his herds and to sacrifice it to the god; but at the time in question there was born a bull of extraordinary beauty and he sacrificed another from among those which were inferior, whereupon Poseidon becoming angry at Minos, caused his wife Pasiphae to [give] birth to the Minotaur, famed in the myth. This creature, they say, was of double form, the upper parts of the body as far as the shoulders being those of a bull and the remaining parts those of a man.

Above: The bull-headed Minotaur awaits his next meal from across the sea.

and when the Athenians reached Crete, she touched the heart of Minos's daughter Ariadne. The fair princess had come to the seaside with her father to watch the arrival of the tribute ship. The instant she saw Theseus step ashore, she fell deeply in love.

That night Ariadne came to the prison where the Athenians lay awaiting their sacrifice. She pledged her love and promised to help Theseus survive the Labyrinth. Ariadne handed the hero a ball of thread, given to her by Daedalus, the master craftsman who had built the Labyrinth. Then she confided the builder's secret for escaping the baffling maze.

The next morning, when the prisoners were cast into the Labyrinth, Theseus tied one end of the string to the entrance. Slowly he made his way through the dark, winding corridors, stepping over the bones of past victims. He heard the rumble of deep, raspy breathing. He felt a wave of heat and smelled the odor of death and decay. Rounding a bend, he saw the powerful man-like body and hideous bull head of the Minotaur. With a roar the beast attacked. The brave hero fought back with his bare hands and sword. Long and grim was their battle. At last, with one mighty sweep of his blade, Theseus beheaded the monster.

Rewinding the thread, Theseus traced his way back through the Labyrinth. Near the entrance he found the other Athenians waiting. Together they fled to the harbor, where they knocked holes in the bot-

The ancient tale of Theseus in the Labyrinth inspired this 4th-century mosaic from a Roman estate in Austria.

THE PERILS *of* PRIDE

Daedalus and Icarus

IN THE WORLD OF GREEK MYTHOLOGY, THE WORST offense a mortal could commit was to challenge the gods. The excessive pride or self-confidence that could make people believe themselves equal to the gods was sometimes called hubris. Men and women might show their hubris by competing with the gods, disobeying their commands, or approaching them without an invitation. Sometimes mortals committed these acts unintentionally. For example, one myth told of a boy named Tiresias, who accidentally caught a glimpse of the goddess Athena while she was bathing in a mountain pool. Tiresias was struck blind for his offense. In other myths people guilty of hubris were skinned alive, wiped out by a thunderbolt, or turned into a rock or a spider.

Opposite: An 18th-century marble statue shows the crafty inventor Daedalus outfitting his beloved son Icarus with wings.

trembling voice the fond father urged his son to stay close. With tears rolling down his aged cheeks, he told Icarus not to fly too low or the waves would wet his wings, not too high or the sun would melt the wax. Wrapping the child in his arms, he kissed the smooth young brow. Then Daedalus stepped out into the open air and, like a baby bird leaving its nest for the first time, Icarus followed.

Northward over the blue Aegean Sea the pair flew. They passed the islands of Paros and Delos. They passed Samos, center for the worship of Hera, proud queen of the Olympians. As they glided over the coast of that fair isle, a fisherman gazed up in wonder and a shepherd dropped his staff. A plowman in his fields breathed a prayer, mistaking the great winged creatures for gods.

All this time young Icarus had heeded his father's warning and kept to the middle air. But as the pair soared through the wide-open skies, the boy began to long for greater heights. In his excitement he grew wild and careless. Boldly he climbed, higher and higher, as if reaching for heaven itself. Icarus felt the burning anger of Helios the sun god on his back. Ignoring the warning, he climbed still higher. Soon he felt a warm trickle down his shoulders as Helios caused the wax to melt. One by one his feathers loosened and scattered on the breeze. In vain Icarus beat his faltering wings. Crying out to his father, he tumbled from on high and vanished in the deep blue sea. Hearing the boy's cries, Daedalus hurried back. Again and again the father, now a father no more, called out for his son. Then Daedalus saw the feathers scattered over the waves and cursed the cleverness that had led to his fatal invention. Circling over the

Helios, the sun god, on an ancient Greek silver coin

OH! FATHER, FATHER, AS HE STROVE TO CRY,
DOWN TO THE SEA HE TUMBLED FROM ON HIGH.

— OVID, 1ST CENTURY CE

water, he recovered the body of his poor drowned son. He buried Icarus on a nearby island, which he named Icaria in the boy's memory. The sea where Icarus fell has been known ever since as the Icarian Sea.

Some say that Daedalus journeyed on safely to Sicily, where he earned riches and fame in the court of the king. Others report that the grieving father landed in Cumae, in southern Italy. There he built a temple to Apollo and hung up his magical wings, as a sad offering to the god of light and science.

Bellerophon prepares to ride the marvelous winged horse Pegasus into battle.

BELLEROPHON *and* PEGASUS

Another myth warning mortals against excessive pride was the tale of Bellerophon (buh-LER-uh-fon) and the winged horse Pegasus. Bellerophon was a hero who performed incredible deeds while riding the magical horse. He killed a fire-breathing monster called the Chimera (kie-MER-uh), and he defeated a race of fierce female warriors known as the Amazons. Bellerophon's victories made him so arrogant that he decided to ride Pegasus to Mount Olympus and join the gods. To punish the man's hubris, Zeus sent a horsefly to sting the flying horse. Bellerophon was thrown to the earth, where he spent the rest of his days lame and blind. Here the Greek poet Pindar explains how Bellerophon tamed Pegasus with a magical bridle, given to him by the goddess Athena, and then rode the steed to glory.

As [Bellerophon] slumbered in the darkness . . . the daughter herself of Zeus whose spear is the thunderbolt . . . brought to him a bridle with golden cheek-pieces. . . . He seized the marvelous thing that lay beside him [and] eagerly stretched the gentle charmed bridle around [Pegasus's] jaws and caught the winged horse. Mounted on its back and armored in bronze, at once he began to play with weapons. And with Pegasus, from the chilly bosom of the lonely air, he once attacked the Amazons, the female army of archers, and he killed the fire-breathing Chimera. . . . I shall pass over his death in silence; but Pegasus has found his shelter in the ancient stables of Zeus in Olympus.

The **TROJAN WAR**

The Judgment of Paris
AND
The Trojan Horse

THE GREATEST OF ALL GREEK HEROIC MYTHS WAS THE story of the Trojan War. This epic adventure tale had something for everyone: love, hate, loyalty, betrayal, courage, cowardice, birth, death, triumph, and tragedy. It explored issues of great importance to the people of ancient Greece, including honor, glory, the perils of angering the gods, and the inescapable nature of fate. The Greeks also valued the story because they regarded the Trojan War as a turning point in their history, the first time they came together as one people united in a common cause.

Like many Greek myths, the story of the Trojan War may have been inspired by real events in the distant past. Archaeologists have uncovered part of the ruins of the ancient city of Troy on the western coast of modern-day Turkey. They have found evidence of major military

Opposite: Helen of Troy, daughter of Zeus and a mortal queen, was the most beautiful woman in the world.

conflicts between the Trojans and invading armies, who may have included the Mycenaean Greeks. For centuries Greek storytellers passed down the history of those conflicts orally, through their poetry and song. The first written version of the tale appeared in the epic poems the *Iliad* and the *Odyssey,* composed by Homer around the second half of the eighth century BCE. By that time, memories of the Trojan War had been transformed into a complex mythological narrative involving hundreds of superhuman heroes and gods.

According to mythology, the Trojan War began when Paris, prince of Troy, abducted Helen, the beautiful queen of a Greek city-state. To recover Helen and punish the Trojans, the Greeks launched the greatest expedition ever known. For nine years Greek armies assaulted the walled city of Troy and the surrounding territories. During this long campaign, some of the Olympian gods and goddesses actively supported the Greeks, while others sided with the Trojans. In the tenth year the Greeks came up with a plan for entering Troy and winning the war.

An ancient sculptor's portrayal of the great Greek poet Homer

The story of the Trojan War has stirred the imagination of countless writers and artists, from Homer all the way through the present day. Our retelling focuses on the two myths that open and close that epic tale. "The Judgment of Paris" presents the incident that led to the abduction of Helen. "The Trojan Horse" tells of the clever plan that brought about the Greeks' final victory.

CAST *of* CHARACTERS

Eris Goddess of strife, or conflict

Hera (HER-uh) Queen of the Olympians

Athena (uh-THEE-nuh) Goddess of war and wisdom

Aphrodite (af-ruh-DIE-tee) Goddess of love and beauty

Zeus (zoos) King of the Olympians

Hermes (HER-meez) Messenger of the gods

Paris Son of Priam

Priam (PRIE-um) King of Troy

Hecuba (HEH-kyuh-buh) Wife of Priam

Helen Queen of Sparta; also known as Helen of Troy

Odysseus (oh-DIH-see-us) Famous Greek hero; also known as Ulysses

Sinon (SIE-non) Brave Greek soldier

Laocoön (lay-AH-kuh-wan) Trojan priest

The Judgment of Paris

T HE ROOTS OF THE TROJAN WAR reach all the way back to a wedding party on the slopes of Mount Pelion. This was no ordinary wedding, but the union of a mortal king and a lovely sea goddess. All the gods and goddesses were invited to celebrate the grand event.

All, that is, but one. Eris, goddess of strife, was never invited to such joyful gatherings, because of her talent for stirring up trouble.

Unfortunately, Eris showed up anyway. Just as the guests were raising their cups to toast the happy couple, the goddess strolled in with her eyes flashing and her lips curled in a nasty smile. Calmly Eris surveyed the immortals who had snubbed her. There was a sudden flash of light as she rolled a shiny orb at their feet. Then—snap!—she vanished. The crowd gathered around the glittering object. It was a golden apple, inscribed with the words TO THE FAIREST.

In an instant three of the Olympian goddesses—Hera, Athena, and Aphrodite—all reached for the lovely apple. A bitter quarrel broke out, with each goddess claiming that *she* deserved the prize because she was by far the most beautiful. The rivals turned to Zeus, asking him to settle their argument. But the lord of the immortals was no fool. He was not about to take sides in such a delicate matter. Instead, Zeus ordered Hermes to take the three goddesses to a valley near the city of Troy. There a handsome young shepherd named Paris could decide who was the fairest.

COME HERE AND DECIDE WHICH IS THE MORE EXCELLENT BEAUTY OF FACE, AND TO THE FAIRER GIVE THIS APPLE'S LOVELY FRUIT.

◦ COLLUTHUS, 5TH–6TH CENTURIES BCE

Now, Paris was more than a simple herdsman. In fact, he was a prince, the son of King Priam and Queen Hecuba of Troy. Years earlier, while Hecuba carried her unborn son within her, she had dreamed that she would give birth to a flame that would consume the entire city. The royal couple had been horrified by this evil omen. As soon as

Paris was born, they reluctantly handed him to a shepherd, ordering the man to kill the ill-fated infant. The shepherd abandoned the little prince on the barren slopes of Mount Ida. When the man returned five days later, however, he found the child alive and well, nursing from a she-bear. Concluding that the gods must have spared the boy's life for some hidden purpose, the shepherd took Paris home and raised him as his own son.

So it was that Paris, prince of Troy, stood watching over a flock of sheep when Hermes and the three goddesses appeared before him.

The shepherd trembled at the sight of the immortals. But Hermes spoke softly, calming his fears and telling him of the great honor that had been bestowed upon him. In the name of Zeus, the herald commanded Paris to judge which of the golden goddesses was the fairest. Then Hermes rose on his winged sandals and sped away toward the heavens.

Reassured, the young man began to observe the three divine beauties. Each was perfection itself. How could he ever choose a winner? As he pondered the problem, the goddesses offered an array of wondrous gifts to sway his verdict. Hera promised to make the young man ruler of a rich and powerful kingdom if he would name her the fairest. Athena tempted him with wisdom and glory in battle. Last of all, Aphrodite offered the fairest woman in all the world as his wife. And Paris, judging that love was greater than power or glory, awarded the golden apple to Aphrodite.

Hermes, messenger of the gods, in a 16th-century painting by Italian master Raphael

The Trojan Horse

THE JUDGMENT OF PARIS meant disaster for Troy. Shortly after the divine beauty contest, King Priam acknowledged the young shepherd as his son and heir. Paris sailed off to the Greek city-state of Sparta to claim his prize: the most beautiful woman in the world, Helen. With the help of Aphrodite, he persuaded Helen to leave her husband, King Menelaos of Sparta, and elope with him to Troy. That act set off a disastrous war between the Trojans and an invading Greek army.

THE GREEKS SPEAK
HELEN'S LAMENT

Many ancient Greek storytellers denounced Helen for deserting her husband, Menelaos, for Paris, the young prince of Troy. In contrast, Homer presented her as a sympathetic character who, like all mortals, was simply a tool of the gods. In this scene from Homer's *Iliad*, Helen meets King Priam and his counselors on the walls of Troy.

Watching Helen as she climbed the stair [the counselors] said to one another: "We cannot rage at her, it is no wonder that Trojans and [Greeks] under arms should for so long have borne the pains of war for one like this. Unearthliness. A goddess the woman is to look at." . . . To Helen Priam called out: "Come here, dear child, sit here beside me. . . . You are not to blame, I hold the gods to blame for bringing on this war against the [Greeks] to our sorrow. . . . And the great beauty, Helen, replied: "Revere you as I do, I dread you, too, dear father. Painful death would have been sweeter for me, on that day I joined your son, and left my bridal chamber, my brothers, my grown child, my childhood friends! But no death came, though I have pined and wept."

Above: Helen pours wine for King Priam of Troy on an ancient Greek drinking cup.

Year after year the Trojan War dragged on, with many acts of bravery and turns of fortune on both sides. Still, the people of Troy held out inside their walled city. The Greeks, weary of bloodshed and longing for home, began to despair of ever subduing their enemy.

Then Athena, who hated the Trojans because Paris had judged her less beautiful than Aphrodite, whispered a plan to the wily Greek chieftain Odysseus. Under his direction the Greeks built a huge wooden horse with a great hollow belly. One side of the horse held a cunningly concealed door. On the other side was an inscription: FOR THEIR RETURN HOME, THE GREEKS DEDICATE THIS THANK-OFFERING TO ATHENA.

When night fell, Odysseus and fifty armed warriors climbed into the belly of the horse. The rest of the Greeks burned their tents, boarded their ships, and sailed to the far side of a nearby island. Only one man remained. This was a brave soldier named Sinon, who had volunteered to stay behind and allow himself to be captured.

The next morning the Trojans awoke to find the enemy camp deserted and the colossal fleet gone. Throwing open their gates, they poured out of the city to rejoice in their victory and marvel at the giant horse. Some of the Trojans wanted to bring the image inside the city as a trophy. Others, distrusting the monstrous beast, wanted to light a bonfire beneath it. As the two sides argued, a shout arose and a group of shepherds dragged in the Greek soldier Sinon. With much trembling and rolling of eyes, the captive told his false tale. After a quarrel with Odysseus, Sinon said bitterly, he had been left behind to die. As for the wooden horse, that was an offering to Athena, made by his former comrades to ensure favorable winds on their return journey. Then Sinon confided a great secret. The Greeks had purposely made the horse too big to pass through the gates of Troy. For if the Trojans took the sacred image into their city, they would gain mastery over all their enemies.

Hearing Sinon's tale, the Trojans clamored to bring in the wondrous horse. Only the wise priest Laocoön still urged caution. The priest hurled his spear at the wooden beast. He warned his countrymen to beware of gifts from the treacherous Greeks. But as Laocoön spoke, Athena grew angry at his interference. The goddess caused two immense serpents to rise from the sea. Hissing and sputtering flames, the monsters slithered swiftly across the beach. They wrapped their giant coils around Laocoön and his two young sons and choked them to death.

TWO SERPENTS SWAM THROUGH THE SEA FROM THE NEIGHBORING ISLANDS AND DEVOURED THE SONS OF LAOCOÖN.
— APOLLODORUS, 2ND CENTURY BCE

Now fear and amazement seized the Trojans. Many shouted that Athena had sent the serpents to punish the priest for dishonoring her sacred image. Quickly men fastened wheels to the horse's feet and tied ropes around its flanks. Eagerly they pried stones from the city walls to enlarge the gates. Then a throng of the strongest Trojans hauled the unwieldy steed through the gates to a place of honor outside Athena's temple.

Long and loud were the celebrations on that festive occasion. It was the middle of the night before the Trojans finally retired, worn out with wine and merriment. As they slept, the traitor Sinon lit a beacon fire to guide the Greek fleet back to shore. He knocked on the door of the wooden horse to summon the hidden warriors. Silently the soldiers slid down a rope to the street. They unbarred the gates of Troy and admitted their army. Then, marching through the city, the Greeks began to enter the houses and slaughter the Trojans in their beds.

Trumpets rang out, calling the men of Troy to repel the foe. The clash of arms mingled with loud laments, and the streets flowed with blood. A crackling fire, borne by the wind, consumed homes, temples, and palaces. By the break of day, all but a few of the Trojan men had been slain, and the women and children were dead or taken captive.

And what of Helen, whose divine beauty had been the cause of so much misery? She was reunited with Menelaos, the husband she had never ceased to love, even when Aphrodite bewitched her into betraying him for another. Returning to Sparta, the couple lived together happily for many years. And when they died, the gods took them to the Elysian Fields, where they strolled hand in hand forever.

GLOSSARY

ambrosia the food of the Greek gods, which had the power to give immortality to mortals

archaeologists scientists who study the physical remains of past cultures to learn about human life and activity

city-states independent states that were made up of a city and its surrounding territory

deities gods, goddesses, and other divine beings

epic a long narrative poem celebrating the deeds of legendary or historical beings

genealogy a record of the descent of individuals from their ancestors

hubris (HYOO-brus) excessive pride or arrogance; in ancient Greece *hubris* was also a term that referred to the act of taking pleasure in insulting or dishonoring a person

immortal living forever

legend a traditional story that may involve ordinary mortals as well as divine beings and may be partly based on real people and events

Macedonia (ma-suh-DOH-nee-uh) an ancient kingdom on the Balkan Peninsula, centered in a plain north of Mount Olympus, which was ruled by Philip II and his son Alexander the Great

Minoan (muh-NO-un) relating to the people or culture of ancient Crete, beginning around 3000 BCE

minstrels entertainers who traveled from place to place, playing music, singing verses, and reciting poetry

Mycenaean (my-suh-NEE-un) relating to the people or culture of Mycenae (my-SEE-nee), the ancient city that reached its height around 1400 BCE and was the center of the first great civilization of mainland Greece

mythology the whole body of myths belonging to a people

myths traditional stories about gods and other divine and sometimes mortal beings, which were developed by ancient cultures to explain the mysteries of the physical and spiritual worlds

nectar the sweet drink of the Olympian gods

nymphs fairylike beings who were believed to dwell in rivers, pools, trees, and mountains

omen an occurrence that is believed to be a sign of good or bad luck to come

Panhellenic relating to all Greece or all the Greek people

patron deity a god or goddess adopted by a polis as its special protector

polis (PAH-lus) one of the city-states of ancient Greece; the plural is *poleis* (PAH-lays)

pomegranate (PAH-muh-gran-ut) a thick-skinned, reddish fruit with many tart seeds

prophecy a prediction of something to come

Tartarus a deep, sunless region in the lowest part of the underworld

tribute a payment given by one ruler or country to another as a sign of respect and submission

trident a spear with three prongs

tyrants rulers who took over city-states and established dynasties (hereditary ruling families)

BIOGRAPHICAL DICTIONARY *of* GREEK WRITERS

Following are brief biographies of the ancient Greek poets, playwrights, historians, and other writers mentioned in this book.

Aeschylus (ESS-kuh-lus) *525–456* BCE

The playwright Aeschylus is often called the father of Greek tragedy. He is believed to have written about ninety plays, but only seven have survived. His best-known plays were tragedies, or serious dramas describing a conflict between the main character and a larger force such as fate. Aeschylus's tragedies included *Prometheus Bound,* the story of the Titan honored as the champion of humankind, and *Agamemnon,* the tale of a Greek hero's disastrous return from the Trojan War.

Apollodorus *around 2nd century* BCE

The Greek scholar Apollodorus is most famous for his *Chronicle*, a history of Greece from the legendary fall of Troy in the eleventh century BCE to 144 BCE. He also wrote several works on grammar and mythology.

Colluthus *5th–6th centuries* BCE

Colluthus of Lycopolis was a Greek poet known for his one surviving work, *The Rape of Helen*. This epic poem recounts the events leading up to the Trojan War, from the Judgment of Paris to the "rape," or abduction, of Helen from Sparta.

Diodorus Siculus *around 90–21* BCE

This Greek historian wrote the *Bibliotheca Historica*, or *Library of History*, a forty-volume work claiming to cover the history of the entire world from the creation through the early years of the Roman Empire. Diodorus's ambitious work was drawn from his extensive travels and from the writings of earlier historians.

Hesiod *8th century* BCE

The poet Hesiod is known mainly for two long poems, *Theogony*, or "Genealogy of the Gods," and *Works and Days*. *Theogony* draws on earlier traditional tales to tell the story of the creation of the world and the birth of the gods. *Works and Days* offers advice on moral living and the importance of honest work. It is the first known didactic poem, which means that it was intended to be educational or instructive rather than simply entertaining.

Homer *9th–8th centuries* BCE

Homer is traditionally considered the composer of the two most important epic poems from ancient Greece, the *Iliad* and the *Odyssey*. The *Iliad* is set in the last year of the Trojan War, and the *Odyssey* describes the long homeward journey of the heroic Greek warrior Odysseus. Some scholars believe that one or both of the epics may actually be collections of works by several different poets.

Pindar *around 522–438* BCE

Pindar is often called Greece's greatest writer of lyric poetry, or songlike poems meant to be chanted or sung. Most of his surviving poems were composed in honor of the victors at the Olympian Games and other national festivals.

Plato *around 428–348* BCE

The Greek philosopher Plato is considered one of the most important and influential thinkers of the Western world. He founded one of the first universities, the Academy in Athens. Plato wrote a series of dialogues, which presented philosophical ideas in the form of conversations between two or more people. His best-known work was the *Republic,* a dialogue exploring the meaning and value of justice.

Plutarch (PLOO-tark) *around 46–120* CE

The writer Plutarch is best known for his *Parallel Lives,* also known as *Plutarch's Lives,* a series of biographies comparing the lives of famous Greeks and Romans. Along with well-researched historical information, the biographies explored the influence of the subjects' character on their lives and destinies. Plutarch also wrote on such topics as morality, religion, and philosophy.

To FIND OUT MORE

BOOKS

Ashworth, Leon. *Gods and Goddesses of Ancient Greece.* North Mankato, MN: Smart Apple Media, 2003.

Barber, Antonia. *Apollo and Daphne: Masterpieces of Mythology.* Los Angeles, CA: J. Paul Getty Museum, 1998.

Bolton, Lesley. *The Everything Classical Mythology Book.* Avon, MA: Adams Media, 2002.

Daly, Kathleen N. *Greek and Roman Mythology A to Z.* Revised edition. New York: Facts on File, 2004.

D'Aulaire, Ingri, and Edgar Parin D'Aulaire. *D'Aulaires' Book of Greek Myths.* Garden City, NY: Doubleday, 1995.

Evslin, Bernard. *Heroes, Gods and Monsters of the Greek Myths.* New York: Four Winds Press, 1999.

Hamilton, Edith. *Mythology: Timeless Tales of Gods and Heroes.* New York: Warner Books, 1999.

Houle, Michelle M. *Gods and Goddesses in Greek Mythology.* Berkeley Heights, NJ: Enslow, 2001.

Nardo, Don. *Greek Mythology.* San Diego, CA: KidHaven Press, 2002.

WEB SITES*

The Ancient Gods at http://www.hol.gr/greece/ancgods.htm
This site from Hellas On Line offers brief biographies and a family tree of the Greek gods and goddesses.

Classical Myth: The Ancient Sources at
http://web.uvic.ca/grs/bowman/myth/index.html
Designed by the University of Victoria in British Columbia, Canada, this very useful site presents ancient texts and images relating to the Olympian gods. Also included is a time line of Greek history and literature.

Encyclopedia Mythica at
http://www.pantheon.org/areas/mythology/europe/greek/articles.html
This online encyclopedia contains hundreds of articles on the gods, goddesses, heroes, and legendary creatures of ancient Greece.

Windows to the Universe, World Mythology, at
http://www.windows.ucar.edu/tour/link=/mythology/worldmap_new.html
Created by the University of Michigan, this excellent site gives visitors a choice of text presented at beginning, intermediate, or advanced levels. Click on the word *Greek* on the world map for information and art relating to the Greek gods and heroes.

* All Internet sites were available and accurate when this book was sent to press.

World Myths and Legends in Art at
  http://www.artsmia.org/world-myths/artbyculture/greek.html
  The Minneapolis Institute of Arts presents this collection of works
  of art inspired by Greek and Roman myths. The site includes images
  of ancient and modern-day paintings and sculptures, along with
  summaries of the myths, background information on culture, and
  discussion questions.

SELECTED BIBLIOGRAPHY

Avery, Catherine B., ed. *The New Century Handbook of Greek Mythology
  and Legend.* New York: Appleton-Century-Crofts, 1972.
Bulfinch, Thomas. *The Golden Age of Myth and Legend.* Hertfordshire,
  England: Wordsworth Reference, 1993.
Buxton, Richard. *The Complete World of Greek Mythology.* London:
  Thames and Hudson, 2004.
Cotterell, Arthur. *Classical Mythology.* New York: Lorenz Books, 2000.
Diodorus Siculus. *Library of History.* Vol. 3. Translated by C. H.
  Oldfather. Cambridge, MA: Harvard University Press, 1985.
Field, D. M. *Greek and Roman Mythology.* New York: Chartwell Books, 1977.
Hesiod. *Theogony.* Translated by Norman O. Brown. Indianapolis:
  Bobbs-Merrill, 1953.
———. *Works and Days and Theogony.* Translated by Stanley Lombardo.
  Indianapolis, IN: Hackett Publishing, 1993.
Homer. *The Iliad.* Translated by Robert Fitzgerald. Garden City, NY:
  Doubleday, 1974.
———. *The Odyssey.* Translated by Robert Fitzgerald. Garden City, NY:
  Doubleday, 1961.
Kokkinou, Sophia. *Greek Mythology.* Athens, Greece: Intercarta, 1989.
Murray, Alexander S. *Manual of Mythology.* Edited by William H.
  Klapp. New York: Tudor, 1935.
Schmidt, Joel. *Larousse Greek and Roman Mythology.* Edited by Dr. Seth
  Benardete. New York: McGraw-Hill, 1980.

Souli, Sofia A. *Greek Mythology*. Ilioupoli, Greece: Editions Michalis Toubis, 1995.

Summers, Kirk. *Greek and Roman Mythology*. Dubuque, IA: Kendall/Hunt Publishing, 2003.

Wright, John Henry, ed. *Masterpieces in Greek Literature*. Freeport, NY: Books for Libraries, 1970.

NOTES *on* QUOTATIONS

Quoted passages in sidebars come from the following sources:

"The Birth of Aphrodite," page 34, from Hesiod, *Theogony,* translated by Norman O. Brown (New York: Bobbs-Merrill Company, 1953).

"Why the Gods Get the Bones," page 43, from Hesiod, *Works and Days and Theogony,* translated by Stanley Lombardo (Indianapolis, IN: Hackett, 1993).

"The Kingdom of Hades," page 50, from Plato, *Gorgias,* translated by Benjamin Jowett, at http://www.ancienttexts.org/library/greek/plato/gorgias.html

"The Temple of Demeter," page 53, from the *Homeric Hymn to Demeter,* translated by Hugh G. Evelyn-White, at http://www.sacred-texts.com/cla/demeter.htm

"The Glory of Hercules," page 61, from *Plutarch's Lives: Theseus,* translated by John Dryden, at http://classics.mit.edu/Plutarch/theseus.html

"The Birth of the Minotaur," page 64, from Diodorus Siculus, *Library of History,* vol. 3, translated by C. H. Oldfather (Cambridge, MA: Harvard University Press, 1985).

"Bellerophon and Pegasus," page 75, from Pindar, *Odes,* "Olympian XIII," at *The Perseus Digital Library,* translated by Basil L. Gildersleeve and Anne Mahoney, at http://www.perseus.tufts.edu

"Helen's Lament," page 83, from Homer, *The Iliad,* translated by Robert Fitzgerald (Garden City, NY: Doubleday, 1974).

INDEX
Page numbers for illustrations are in boldface

ABOUT *the* AUTHOR

"I can't think of a better way to learn about the people of ancient cultures than by reading the stories that held their deepest hopes and fears, their most cherished values and beliefs. While collecting these sacred tales, I looked for the elements that set each culture apart: the special music of the language, the differing roles of men and women, the unique ways of interpreting the mysteries of life. I also enjoyed discovering the many feelings and experiences that unite all peoples around the world, both past and present. Pueblo storyteller Harold Littlebird said it best: 'We know we all come from story. They may not all be the same story but there is a sameness. There is a oneness in it all.' "

VIRGINIA SCHOMP has written more than sixty titles for young readers on topics including dolphins, dinosaurs, occupations, American history, and world history. Ms. Schomp earned a Bachelor of Arts degree in English Literature from Penn State University. She lives in the Catskill Mountain region of New York with her husband, Richard, and their son, Chip.